FAMILY CONVERSATIONS WE MUST HAVE BUT DO NOT WANT TO

Interactive Planning Workbook for Yourself, Parents, and Grandparents. This Interactive workbook is for anyone over 18 years of age. This interactive workbook also covers the topic of Long-Term Care and the options available for care...

Michael White LNHA, LALD and Lisa White RN

Dedication

This book is dedicated to my family; my wife, who is a registered nurse, and our first son, who is an internal medicine resident physician. Our second daughter who elected a different route other than medicine but shows compassion and care daily to those she interacts with as a buyer for a major corporation, she will soon be a great mother. Our third child is an OB/GYN resident physician, and our youngest son is a physician assistant student. Thank you all for supporting this effort and pushing me to finish this workbook. You all see first-hand what people and families go through when medical conditions change, and when they are unprepared to make these decisions, some can be easy decisions and some extremely difficult decisions.

Preface

I have spent the majority of my years working in the medical profession, and I currently have studied and tested to acquire my Nursing Home Administration License and Assisted Living License. I have another 3 years selling Nursing Home Insurance to seniors, of which most of them inevitably stated, "I will never need long-term care in my life." These are the comments that inspired me to write this interactive workbook because most of us will need to plan and make decisions, whether it be for acute illnesses, chronic illnesses or for long-term care choices.

My desire is that families will take time to complete this workbook and make changes and amendments to the workbook as their healthcare needs change or in preparation or planning for life events. As the title of the workbook states, these are conversations that we must have but do not want to. They are not always enjoyable conversations, but they can take the guesswork out of what you want and wish for and reduce stress levels in making healthcare decisions. For example, many times, Alzheimer's disease or Dementia strikes so fast that those affected by these disease processes cannot verbalize or cognitively think clearly to make decisions for themselves, and the family is the one holding the torch. This workbook is to guide your family along the path that YOU desire. My hope is that this workbook will help families to see the importance and need of finding the answers to the questions that nobody wants to address, but must!

All of us, at one time or another, will experience life events that can bring about change and tough decisions to make about your own health or a loved one's health and sometimes life alone, and these changes can unfortunately begin early in life or as a result of a traumatic injury, or just the progression of growing old.

Throughout my lifetime, I have witnessed families, including my own, needing to make decisions regarding their own health or a family member's health, who are aging or, in my instance, a surgical procedure that went extremely bad. Some of these decisions can be relatively easy, and others become confusing, complicated and difficult. I am a licensed nursing home administrator and a licensed assisted living director, and I have seen first-hand many accounts of uncertainties and questions that families have to make, and because we mostly are unaware of health changes or conditions and begin searching for answers, sometimes, when it is too late. This interactive and informative workbook is designed to help grandparents, parents, children, individuals and spouses of any age, to guide and work through these decisions and questions that are set before them. As our health changes, so do some of these decisions, so this interactive workbook is designed to be amended as these changes occur in our lives. The intent is to help us all answer those tough questions that nobody wants to discuss but that we must at some point in our lives.

PLEASE KEEP THIS INFORMATION SAFE AND ONLY SHARE WITH THOSE YOU ABSOLUTELY TRUST, THIS INFORMATION IS CRITICAL AND VALUABLE, SO PLEASE KEEP THIS IN A SAFE PLACE, AND LET THOSE WHO YOU TRUST KNOW WHERE THIS INTERACTIVE WORKBOOK IS KEPT.

Table of Contents

Let's get started

When should we begin planning as families, and begin discussing why it is important and what purpose does this provide for your family?

Most families going through major changes in health or life, have probably never been guided as to where to begin, and this interactive workbook will help you understand better what information is needed, which will help not only you make decisions, but it will also guide your family in the event your health decisions are questioned. This Interactive Workbook will also define your wishes for your family and those closest to you. Planning for the future while you are healthy is very advantageous and should be taken very seriously. **Keep in mind that this workbook is for anyone over the age of 18 years of age, who can make their own decisions regarding their health care choices and determinations.**

How to use the interactive Workbook: Your information can be written in this book for safekeeping.

Talk with your family and inform them of the planning that you have completed in this workbook or complete this with the guidance of your family. Keep this in a safe place and let your family know where it is located. It is also important that you review this information yearly so that it is kept up to date as your health may or may not change, so we have included a notes/addendum section so that you can make changes as needed. This information will help your family and your medical providers understand what your personal wishes are regarding your health care.

I would like to provide you with a personal scenario to help you understand the importance of this information. In 2018, my 80-year-old mother was scheduled for an outpatient cardiac ablation procedure. The procedure was to last less than one hour, and she was to be discharged an hour or two after the procedure was completed. During the procedure, unfortunately, a complication of the procedure occurred, and she was rushed into the open-heart cardiac operating suite. She underwent open heart surgery, which lasted about 7 hours, as they needed to repair a hole in her left ventricle outflow tract. During this time, blood clots had begun to develop in her heart, and when they got her hooked up to the heart-lung bypass machine and began perfusing her blood, it sent 10-plus areas of blood clots into her brain. She coded (her heart had stopped pumping) 4 different times over a total of 14 minutes. Once stable and recovered from the open-heart procedure, she returned to the surgical intensive care unit for close to one month. A follow-up MRI of her brain, showed these 10-plus areas of strokes, and the electro-cardiologist felt as though we should let her die, because her brain function was not what it had been prior to the events of that day. We elected to give my mother the benefit of the doubt and chose against letting her die. Her short-term memory and long-term memory were gone. She did not know what year it was or what month it was. She lost what seemed like all of her memory, her speech was slurred, and she had vision and trouble walking. One of the biggest challenges that faced us now is that we were unsure of what her wishes were for her care as she did not have an advanced healthcare directive, she had not appointed a Power of Attorney, and we frankly were lost as to where all of her personal information was located, and we could not ask her because she could not answer. Had we asked her these questions a day before her procedure, everything could have been written, and we would have had a clearer picture of where her important information was and had a clearer picture of her healthcare wishes. Over the next couple of months and hundreds of phone calls to doctor offices, dental offices and insurance companies, the puzzle started to come together of my mother's information. As I mentioned early, we elected to keep our mother alive. She is still alive and has lived 5 years so far in a nursing home. In the first year of her nursing home year, I would pick her up almost daily and bring her to our home and work with her to see if we could regain some of her memory and physical strength. After about 6 months of working with her as well as physical and occupational therapists, she began to regain her mind and memory. To this day, she has recovered almost 100%, and we have answered many of the questions that you will complete in this workbook. She now has an advanced directive that describes what her healthcare wishes are, we now have power of attorney signed, and we have a clearer picture of what her desires and legacy look like.

This example is just one of thousands that take place every day that most families are unprepared for and find themselves in the same situation as what my family experienced. This type of planning is invaluable and can alleviate many discrepancies in regard to your healthcare and your personal wishes.

Other Information that is important for your family to know, are your passwords to your cell phone and computers in the event that they need to access that information. I will say that it is important that you share this information with those you trust and keep it in a confidential, safe location. It is also important that you make available Social Security Numbers with those you trust, I would not want you to lose this workbook and have that valuable information in the hands of the wrong person(s).

Personal Health Information

Do you have a Living Will, and if so, please list the location of where the Living Will is kept.

Self: _____

Spouse/Significant Other: _____

Please seek legal advice for setting up a living will or trust.

Notes/Addendums

Do you have an Advanced Directive, and if so, please list the location of where the Advanced Directive is kept. This is important so that family members can refer to what your health care wishes are.

Self: _____

Spouse/Significant Other: _____

Please seek help from your designated state health department for more information regarding Advanced Directives.

Notes/Addendums

8

Please list your date of birth.

Self: _____

Spouse/Significant Other: _____

Social Security numbers (I advise letting those know where that information is and not kept in this book in the event it gets stolen or lost) and Monthly benefit amount?

Self: _____

Social Security Number:

Social Security Monthly Benefit Amount:

Spouse/Significant Other: _____

Social Security Number:

Social Security Monthly Benefit Amount:

Notes/Addendums

Are you a veteran of the military and if so, what branch did you serve.

Self: _____

Spouse/Significant Other: _____

Notes/Addendums

Power of attorney (POA) documents give one or more people the power to act on your behalf as your attorney-in-fact or agent when you aren't able to be there in person or are otherwise mentally incompetent or physically unable to represent yourself. (LEGALZOOM)

Durable powers of attorney help you plan for medical emergencies and declines in mental functioning. Having these documents in place helps eliminate confusion and uncertainty when family members have to step in to handle finances or make tough medical decisions. (LEGAL ZOOM)

FAMILY ADVOCACY- REST ASSURED SOMETIMES THE BEST ADVICE AND INFORMATION COME FROM THOSE WHO LOVE YOU THE MOST, AND IF THERE EVER COMES A TIME THAT YOU NEED HELP MAKING THE RIGHT DECISIONS ABOUT YOUR DESIRES AND HEALTHCARE COORDINATION OF CARE WILL COME FROM THOSE THAT KNOW AND LOVE YOU THE MOST. THE IMPORTANCE OF FAMILY ADVOCACY CANNOT BE STRESSED ENOUGH AT ALL LEVELS OF HEALTHCARE. WHO ARE YOU ADVOCATES ROOTING FOR YOU AND WANTING THE BEST OUTCOME FOR YOU, WHO ARE THOSE TEAM MEMBERS?

Notes/Addendums

15

Do you have a Power of Attorney or a Durable Power of Attorney, if so, please list those designees? Do you have a Designated Representative?

Self: _____

Spouse/Significant Other: _____

Notes/Addendums

17

If you become incapacitated, (quadriplegic, paraplegic, or have a tracheostomy, breathing tube inserted and cannot speak), what are your wishes and does your advanced directive explain this and/or does your Power of Attorney understand your wishes?

Self: _____

Spouse: _____

Significant Other: _____

Notes/Addendums

What are your wishes as far as Code Status? Full Code (Resuscitation), or DNR-Do not resuscitate. Do you want life saving measures implemented if needed?

Self: _____

Significant Other: _____

Notes/Addendums

Do you have an attorney, name and contact information?

    Self: _____

    Attorney Name:

    Address:

    Phone Number:

    Spouse/Significant Other: _____

    Attorney Name:

    Address:

    Phone Number:

Notes/Addendums

Do you have any Trusts in place, revocable or irrevocable? Where is that information Located and who is your attorney and contact information?

Self: _____

Attorney Name:

Address:

Phone Number:

Type of Trust:

Location of Trust Documents:

Spouse/Significant Other: _____

Attorney Name:

Address:

Phone Number:

Type of Trust:

Location of Trust Documents:

Notes/Addendums

Do you have an idea of your current total net worth? These numbers are important to generalize with your POA or DPOA, because the cost of care and health services in a LongTerm Care Facility are expensive, and if you were to need government assistance for your care, it gives your POA/DPOA and good understanding of where your assets are and the amounts that you have to work with.

$ 0- 50,000.00

$ 100,000.00 - 200,000.00

$ 200,000.00 - 300,000.00

$ 300,000.00 - 400,000.00 $ 40,000.00 - 500,000.00

Over $500,000.00

Notes/Addendums

What would you like to do with the proceeds of your home, cars, assets? Do you have beneficiaries listed?

Self: _____

Spouse/Significant Other: _____

Notes/Addendums

Do you have any charitable organizations that you would like to donate to in the event of your death? Do you have a suggested dollar amount, or tangible assets that you would like to donate to?

_____

_____

_____

_____

_____

_____

_____

_____

Notes/Addendums

Are you an organ or tissue donor, it is extremely important to discuss this with your family or loved ones as this is very important to those in need of an organ or tissue. It is also advisable to state whether you wishing to donate your body to science, and if so, is there a medical institution that you have chosen?

Self_____

_____

_____

_____

Spouse/Significant
Other_____

_____

_____

_____

_____

Notes/Addendums

Health Insurance

Health Insurance Information, company and contact numbers?

Self: _____

Health Insurance Company:

Health Insurance Policy Number:

Health Insurance Agent contact information:

Spouse/Significant Other: _____

Health Insurance Company:

Health Insurance Policy Number:

Health Insurance Agent contact information:

Notes/Addendums

Please list your Medicare or Medicaid numbers.

Self: _____

Medicare:

Medicaid:

Spouse/Significant Other: _____

Medicare:

Medicaid:

Notes/Addendums

38

Do you own Long-Term Care Insurance and if so, what is the policy number(s) and the document location.

Self: _____

Insurance Company:

Policy Number:

Insurance Agent:

Spouse/Significant Other: _____

Insurance Company:

Policy Number:

Insurance Agent:

Notes/Addendums

Life Insurance Policy numbers, agents and contact information.

Self: _____

Company:

Policy Numbers:

Agent contact information:

Spouse/Significant Other: _____

Company:

Policy Numbers:

Agent contact information:

Notes/Addendums

Please list your beneficiaries on life insurance policies, Primary and Secondary?

Self: _____

Primary Beneficiaries:

Secondary Beneficiaries:

Spouse/Significant Other: _____

Primary Beneficiaries:

Secondary Beneficiaries:

Notes/Addendums

Do you have Dental insurance, company and policy numbers?

Self: _____

Insurance Company:

Policy Number:

Agent Contact Number:

Spouse/Significant Other: _____

Insurance Company:

Policy Number:

Agent Contact Number:

Notes/Addendums

Immunization records- Flu, Tetanus, Covid-19?

Self:_____

Spouse/Significant Other: _____

Notes/Addendums

Do you have any known allergies?

Self:_____

Spouse/Significant Other: _____

Notes/Addendums

Medication List, dosages and Frequency taken? If you have changes in medications, please update in the note section, in the notes and addendums section in this interactive workbook, or write out a list and put it in one of the available folders.

Self:_____

Spouse/Significant Other: _____

Notes/Addendums

Surgical History? Please list any surgical procedures that you have had.

Self:_____

Spouse/Significant Other: _____

Notes/Addendums

Do you have any metal or implants in your body?

Self:_____

Spouse/Significant Other: _____

Notes/Addendums

Do you have any problems with General Anesthesia? Any Reactions, or Malignant Hyperthermia?

Self:_____

Spouse/Significant Other: _____

Notes/Addendums

Healthcare Providers

Who is your primary care physician and their contact information, name, address and phone numbers.

Self: _____

Primary or Family Physician:

Address:

Phone Numbers:

Spouse/Significant Other: _____

Primary or Family Physician:

Address:

Phone Numbers:

Notes/Addendums

Healthcare Specialists- Cardiology, Internal Medicine, Ear, Nose and Throat, Oncologist, Orthopaedics?

Self:_____

Name of Physician and specialty:

Office number:

Address of Physicians office:

Spouse/Significant Other: _____

Name of Physician and specialty:

Office number:

Address of Physicians office:

Notes/Addendums

Who is your Dentist, name, contact information, address, phone number?

Self: _____

Dentist Name:

Address:

Phone Number:

Spouse/Significant Other: _____

Dentist Name:

Address:

Phone Number:

Notes/Addendums

65

Audiology/Optometry Doctors and contact information.

Self:_____

Audiologist Name:

Audiologist Contact information:

Optometrist Name:

Optometrist Contact information:

Spouse/Significant Other: _____

Audiologist Name:

Audiologist Contact information:

Optometrist Name:

Optometrist Contact information:

Notes/Addendums

67

Other Healthcare professionals you see- Chiropractors, Mental Health Professionals, Physical Therapists, Occupational Therapists and their contact information?

Self: _____

Name of Healthcare Professional:

Office number:

Address of Healthcare Professional office:

Spouse/Significant Other: _____

Name of Healthcare Professional:

Office number:

Address of Healthcare Professional office:

Notes/Addendums

69

What hospital do you prefer in the event of an emergency or for your care?

Self:_____

Hospital Name:

Hospital Address:

Hospital Phone Number:

Spouse/Significant Other: _____

Hospital Name:

Hospital Address:

Hospital Phone Number:

Notes/Addendums

Banking Information

Bank Names, Bank accounts and account numbers. Cash in the home and where it is kept.

Self: _____

Bank Name:

Bank Address:

Bank Phone Number:

Checking Account Number:

Savings Account Number:

Spouse/Significant Other: _____

Bank Name:

Bank Address:

Bank Phone Number:

Checking Account Number:

Savings Account Number:

Notes/Addendums

74

Do you have any accounts that have ACH (Automatic monthly payments)withdrawals? Companies and contact information?

Self: _____

Spouse/Significant Other: _____

Notes/Addendums

Monthly, Quarterly, Semi-Annual, Annual Bills, Cell Phones, Utilities? And the amounts owed?

Self: _____

Cell Phone Provider-

Monthly bill-

Cable TV Provider-

Monthly Bill-

Internet Provider-

Monthly Bill-

Utility Company and Monthly Bills-

Other Monthly Bills-

Spouse/Significant Other: _____

Cell Phone Provider-

Monthly bill-

Cable TV Provider-

Monthly Bill-

Internet Provider-

Monthly Bill-

Utility Company and Monthly Bills-

Other Monthly Bills-

Notes/Addendums

Do you have a pension from your employer and the monthly benefit amount and worth?

Self: _____

Company:

Address:

Phone number:

Monthly Benefit Amount:

Spouse/Significant Other: _____

Company:

Address:

Phone number:

Monthly Benefit Amount:

Notes/Addendums

Do you have a Safety deposit box- Keys and location?

Self: _____

Spouse/Significant Other: _____

Notes/Addendums

Do you have a safe at home, how can it be accessed to open it? Keys or Passwords?

Self: _____

Spouse/Significant Other: _____

Notes/Addendums

Do you own, or are you a business partner in any Limited Liability or Business Corporations?

Self: _____

Spouse/Significant Other: _____

Notes/Addendums

Personal Property

Do you own any other property and if so where are the documents showing ownership, and the location of property?

Self: _____

Spouse/Significant Other: _____

Notes/Addendums

Precious metals or other valuables that you own and where are they kept? Collections of valuables?

Self: _____

Spouse/Significant Other: _____

Notes/Addendums

Do you have certain personal items or property that is designated for a specified person or persons or family members? Having this information can prevent family disputes and anger.

Self: _____

Spouse/Significant Other: _____

Notes/Addendums

What certain personal belongings should go to who? This is very important as we have all heard of family arguments over who gets what, please talk this over. Is anything earmarked for family members, friends, churches, charities.

Self: _____

Spouse/Significant Other: _____

Notes/Addendums

Do you own your home? Is your home paid in full? Do you have a second Mortgage?

Self: _____

Spouse: _____

Significant Other: _____

Notes/Addendums

Do you have a Monthly Mortgage and amount? Mortgage Company, account number, and contact information? Do you know what the payoff amount is on your home?

Self: _____

Mortgage Company:

Mortgage Company Address:

Mortgage Company Phone Number:

Mortgage Loan Number:

Spouse/Significant Other: _____

Mortgage Company:

Mortgage Company Address:

Mortgage Company Phone Number:

Mortgage Loan Number:

Notes/Addendums

Do you own any other homes or cabins or rental properties, Timeshares or Land? If so, do you have documentation for those additional homes, mortgages, mortgage loan numbers, and mortgage company contact information? Are they paid in full or do you know the payoff amounts?

Self: _____

Mortgage Company:

Mortgage Company Address:

Mortgage Company Phone Number:

Mortgage Loan Number:

Location of Cabin or Additional Home:

Spouse/Significant Other: _____

Mortgage Company:

Mortgage Company Address:

Mortgage Company Phone Number:

Mortgage Loan Number:

Location of Cabin or Additional Home:

Notes/Addendums

Vehicles owned; Cars, Snowmobiles, Boats, ATV's, Motorcycles, and Location of the Titles, and do any of your cars have loans or liens against them?

      Loan or Lien Company Name:

      Address of Loan or Lien Company:

      Loan Numbers:

Self: _____

Spouse: _____

Significant Other: _____

Notes/Addendums

Automotive Insurance policy numbers, agent and contact information?

Self: _____

Company:

Policy Numbers:

Agent contact information:

Significant Other: _____

Company:

Policy Numbers:

Agent contact information:

Notes/Addendums

Do you have Pets, and who is your Veterinarian and contact information and Pet vaccination records?

Self: _____

Veterinarian Name:

Veterinarian Address:

Veterinarian Phone Number:

Veterinarian Pet Records:

Spouse/Significant Other: _____

Veterinarian Name:

Veterinarian Address:

Veterinarian Phone Number:

Veterinarian Pet Records:

Notes/Addendums

107

CARE OPTIONS AND CARE CONCERNS AS YOU AGE, AS HEALTH NEEDS CHANGE.

Trust your Instincts and be prepared for these signs

Do you see any changes that may be affecting your loved one(s) that you feel need your attention? The following list are triggers for you to consider when you begin to question how your loved one(s) doing living on their own. This is not an exhaustive list, but will give you some ideas of what to be watchful for. These things can change gradually or suddenly, so the important factor is you recognize some of these suggestions.

1. Are medications being taken, and are they taking the medicine at the correct time and the correct dosage? How will you know this?
2. Do they seem lonely or not themselves?
3. Are they taking care of themselves, such as personal hygiene, bathing or showering, and brushing their teeth?
4. Have they fallen and or mentioned that walking, sleeping or getting in and out of bed are difficult tasks?
5. Are they dressing themselves and doing their own laundry?
6. Are they emptying their garbage and getting it out to be picked up by the garbage company?
7. Have their sleeping patterns changed?
8. Are they safe to drive a car to run errands, and are they returning home safely?
9. Is their home being kept up with housecleaning, vacuuming, and dishes being cleaned?
10. Are they able to take care of their finances, bills, and investments?
11. Is the environment that they are living in safe and uncluttered? Are there any tripping hazards that need to be removed?
12. Are they able to get groceries and take proper care of them?
13. Are they becoming forgetful about where they put things, or are they telling you the same stories without remembering telling you?

CAREGIVER BURNOUT IS REAL!!

Another important decision that most of us will make when the time comes will be having family or friends help with the care of a loved one. As great and helpful as this will feel, there are obstacles to this actually happening in the long term. Caregiving for a loved one is very stressful and challenging. The questions that need to be addressed as they relate to caring for your loved one alone or with the help of family are:

1. Do you work, and how will you be able to remain working when you need to provide care to your loved one?

2. Do your relatives and friends work, and how will they be able to do both caregiving and hold down a job?

3. What does it look like when you need to feed, dress and help bathe a loved one? These boundaries are not as easy as you think for both parties involved. There is a sense of privacy and acknowledgement in seeing a loved one undressed, and how do you think they may feel?

4. Have you considered helping a loved one to the restroom and how difficult that may be?

5. How will you handle getting up in the middle of the night to tend to the care that is needed by your loved one, this can happen several times a night.

6. Do you have time to take them to doctor's appts?

7. Do you have time to grocery shop for them?

8. Have you considered living arrangements? Will you be moving in with them, or will they be moving in with you?

9. Can you manage their finances and bills?

10. What are your plans if you want to go away for a weekend or even a vacation for a week or two?

11. How will you feel if you cannot get any support from other family members and you feel that you are doing everything for your loved one?

12. How will you feel if there comes a time when you have to tell them that you can no longer take care of them?

13. As you see, caregiving is a very challenging task and can lead to an increase in emotional and physical stress that can take a toll on you and your family members. Depending on the circumstance, it can be done without many challenges, but truthfully, there are so many things to consider before jumping in and then wondering what did I got myself into. It is very challenging.

<u>What would it look like if you or your family became the sole providers for your loved one(s)?</u>

I have heard many stories from adult children whose parents or grandparents are getting to the point that their health has declined so rapidly that they find themselves searching for answers to questions that they either do not have because of a lack of knowledge, or because some of these issues can be difficult to manage.

Some of the discussions that I have had as a professional in the Long-Term Care sector, are primarily focused on the types of care available to their loved one, and the other big question is who pays for this and what if my parents or grandparents cannot afford to privately pay for their care. As I have defined previously, there are several types of care that can be given, such as Home Care, Assisted Living, Memory Care units and lastly Skilled Nursing Facilities. Typically, families at one time or another either have had friends or relatives receiving these types of care, so that gives them a base for beginning their research on these care services that are provided. Searching within the communities in which the loved one lives is a great place to begin. Contacting local county senior support services or contacting the Department of Health in the State in which you live, will also get you pointed in the right direction. In some circumstances, they can provide you with options for care after you give them some simple background regarding the health care concerns of your loved one. In my experience, as I was looking into Home Health Care for a loved one, they had a registered nurse come to my home to do an assessment and then take that information back to their office and devise a plan for the care needed by my loved one. It takes some effort on your part, and can be confusing and challenging at times, but remember that there are advocacy groups within states and local counties to help guide you.

Financial concern regarding health care is also a hurdle that can be challenging, but when following the continuum of care as health continues to decline and more nursing services are needed, costs rise as it takes more effort and more trained healthcare professionals to help manage the plan of care.

The following are guidelines to follow financially:

A) Most individuals- Over 65 years of age, have Medicare A and Medicare B, keep in mind that Medicare covers hospital and clinic visits in conjunction with the Medicare supplement policy if they have one. It is important to note that Medicare does not cover the costs of nursing home care, although they do have parameters set to cover skilled care for up to 100 days, but after that period of time, you will begin paying out of pocket. There are other parameters within Medicare that if you need additional skilled care, you would need to qualify for, but again, only up to 100 days after you have been diagnosed with a new medical condition.

B) Long-Term Care Insurance - This type of insurance can help you pay for Home healthcare, assisted living, Memory care and skilled nursing communities. The main concern here is that you need to read the fine details of the policies that are being sold today. Some have a waiting period before benefits begin, some have defined per day dollar amounts paid, and the other factor is how long the policy is in effect, 1 year, 3 years, 5 years, or some will pay for a lifetime, although some policies have a maximum amount that will be paid. It is also recommended that if you are needing care, to clarify with the community you will be going if they will accept long-term care insurance.

C) Private pay is the one area that seems to be the easiest to set up for the type of care you need, and most long-term care providers love those who will be paying privately. Paying for long-term care is expensive and typically based on the health services that you need, so keep in mind that in most circumstances, you will be not only paying for rent, but you will be paying for those providing health care services, which are typically defined by the registered nurse who works for the community in which you will be living. Some of these costs can be anywhere from 5000.00 up to 11,000-12,000.00 per month, based on your geographic location. As you can already tell, money goes quickly, and we need to stay on top of these finances. It is also important that you communicate and financial concerns once your finances begin to dip below the 80,000.00 mark. It is also imperative that when you move into a community, you get yourself on the waitlist in the event you spend your assets down and need to begin thinking about state aid programs.

D) Medicaid and Elderly Waiver- Medicaid and Elderly Waiver programs are designed to assist those financially with their care in the event that you do not own assets or have spent your assets on your or your spouse's care. I would highly advise looking into what those program details are, how you qualify, and who you submit paperwork to. Most states have local county assistance to help manage the process of applying and becoming approved for these provided health care service programs. This guide is intended to help you think about these issues and how to navigate these processes. These, again, are generalizations and are dealt with differently in each state, so I would advise contacting the state in which you live.

E)   Medicaid's Look-Back Period Explained- This can become very complicated so please be advised to visit with you attorney or the state assistance programs designated for the state in which you live.

F)   When a senior applies for long-term care Medicaid, whether that be services in one's home, an assisted living residence, or a nursing home, there is an asset (resource) limit. To be eligible for Medicaid, one cannot have assets greater than the limit. Medicaid's Look-Back Period is meant to prevent Medicaid applicants from gifting assets, including selling them under fair market value, to meet Medicaid's asset limit.

G) All asset transfers within the Look-Back Period are reviewed by the Medicaid agency. This includes transfers made by an applicant's spouse. If the Look-Back Rule has been violated, a Penalty Period of Medicaid ineligibility will be established. This is because had the assets not been outright gifted or sold under their fair market value. They could have been used to pay for the elderly individual's long-term care. Note that assets transferred prior to the Look-Back Period are not penalized.

H) The Look-Back Period begins on the date of one's Medicaid application for long-term care. Generally speaking, the "look back" is 60-months (5 years). As an example, a Florida resident applies for Medicaid on Jan. 1, 2023; their Look-Back Period extends back to Dec. 31, 2017. All financial transactions between these dates are subject to review.

I) Examples of transactions that violate the Look-Back Period and could result in penalization include the following: Money gifted to a granddaughter for her high school graduation, a house transferred to a nephew, collectors' coins sold for half their value, and a vehicle donated to a local charity. Additionally, payments made to a personal care assistant without a formal Personal Care Agreement can violate the Look-Back Period.

J) Even after the "initial" Look-Back Period, if a Medicaid beneficiary comes into some money, say, for example, via an inheritance, and gives all (or some) of the money away, they are in violation of the Look-Back Rule. This means that despite an initial determination that one has not violated the 60-month Look-Back Period and is receiving long-term care Medicaid, they can violate this rule, and, hence, be disqualified from Medicaid benefits.

https://www.medicaidplanningassistance.org/medicaid-look-back-period/

Most aging seniors prefer to live in their own homes for as long as they can safely and securely do so. Although staying in your own home would be the best possible scenario, there may come a time when, due to health concerns, we have to make decisions contrary to your wishes of staying in your own home. The comment, "I will never leave my own home to be cared for, or I will never end up in a nursing home" has been said many times, but inevitably, these things sometimes do not leave any other options. Many times, those questions are often left for your family and loved ones to decide. There have been instances when Alzheimer's or Dementia related conditions have overcome our ability to clearly make decisions for ourselves, and this is where things get tricky for families. Children begin to ask questions of each other as to what mom or dad, grandma and grandpa really would want if they weren't overcome with this serious disease process. Is Home Care a viable option? If they are allowed to stay at home, who will check on them hourly, daily, to make sure safety is truly thought out? Will they try to drive their car and get lost, will they go for a walk outside in the middle of the winter and not be able to find their way back home, or will they leave a stove burner on and start a fire? All of these questions need to be carefully thought out to protect the safety of their loved ones.

Would an assisted living facility be the best option, where the community in which you choose can help with daily checks, medication management, food service programs and activities suited for their enjoyment and that will keep their minds active? Assisted Living communities with Memory Care can be of great value for those who have cognitive deficits. In those types of communities, the doors are locked at all times, and only those with granted access are allowed in and out. Meals, activities and apartments are available so that those residents are kept safe and secure. These types of communities also give families the confidence in knowing that their loved one will be taken care of in the best possible way. Caregivers and nurses are consistently in those communities 24 hours a day, 7 days a week.

There are many great options available, and it is through your research in the community in which you live, that you may be able to find what is most appropriate for your loved one. Take time to do your homework, tour facilities, talk to friends and family about any experiences that they may have, and have them share what they liked and disliked about those facilities. It is also important to look at the pricing of these types of care and make sure that when you are comparing the facilities, you are comparing apples to apples, because many of the facilities can have either slight differences or major differences that could affect your decision and how affordable these options are for your loved one.

Long Term Care Expectations

What are your expectations for your care? If your health declines, where would you like to be taken care of? What areas of concern regarding your care can you share?

Self: _____

Spouse/Significant Other: _____

Notes/Addendums

Long Term Care Options

Types of care for seniors - Independent Living, Home Healthcare, assisted living, assisted Living with Alzheimer's and Dementia Care, and Nursing homes.

Activities of Daily Living or ADL's- What are they, and why are they so important?

There are 5 activities of daily living (ADL's) that we all utilize every day from the time we wake up in the morning until the time we go to bed. As we age, there will come a time when those ADL's become very difficult tasks for some seniors. Healthcare providers use ADL's as a way to determine what level of care that you will potentially need or presently need, and then they can devise a plan of care to aid those who are having trouble completing those ADL's.

The 5 ADL's are:

1. Personal Hygiene or Grooming
2. Dressing yourself
3. Toileting
4. Transferring from Chair Standing or Chair to Bed, or even getting out of bed or into bed. Ambulating also falls into this category, can you walk with or without assistance such as another person, a walker, or do you need a wheelchair?
5. Eating- Can you sufficiently cook or prepare food for yourself and feed yourself?

Home Health Care-

Home health care is a wide range of health care services that can be given in your home for an illness or injury. Home health care is usually less expensive, more convenient, and just as effective as care you get in a hospital or skilled nursing facility (SNF). (MEDICARE.GOV)

Adult Day Care:

Adult daycare centers and programs provide a safe, secure setting for older adults who need supervision during the day or who would benefit from additional social engagement outside their homes.

There are more than 7,500 adult day care centers in the U.S. that provide services to older adults, according to the National Adult Day Services Association (NADSA)[1]. For participants, adult daycare programs provide social interaction, mental stimulation, physical activities and nutritious meals. Some offer health services as well. For family caregivers, adult day care centers offer a break from constant caregiving duties and enable them to continue working without worrying about their loved one's safety. (FORBES.COM)

Independent Living- Independent living refers to a wide range of residential options that afford older adults the opportunity to live on their own while taking advantage of various amenities and community offerings. Independent living residential options are usually designed and arranged specifically for older adults, and the type of housing they provide—from apartments to townhomes to single-family homes. (Forbes)

Assisted Living-Assisted living communities are for older adults who want to remain independent in a home-like setting but need non-medical assistance with activities of daily living (ADLs), such as eating, bathing, dressing, maintaining good hygiene and toileting. The person in assisted living typically pays monthly rent for a private apartment or room and an additional fee for the level of care needed.

Residents generally have access to shared common areas. Depending on the community, shared areas may include dining and activity rooms, a cinema room, a library, a pool walking trails or other nature settings on the grounds. Assisted living communities range from those offering basics like daily meals and activities to those with luxury accommodations and amenities, such as spas and bars.

Assisted living communities are typically equipped with 24-hour on-site staff and provide up to three prepared meals a day, as well as housekeeping and some transportation services. (Forbes)

Assisted Living with Alzheimer's or Dementia Care

Memory Care - Memory care facilities are secured facilities that cater to the needs of people with some form of dementia. "Memory care facilities typically have smaller bedrooms but more available, open and inviting common spaces," says Snow.

Research shows the way memory care facilities are designed can be helpful in easing the stressful transition from home to a long-term care community. Softer colors, lack of clutter and clear signage are common therapeutic touches in memory care.

"Confusion and loss of memory can cause anxiety, and having a predictable routine can help ease it," says Pope. "As dementia progresses, they may forget how to do normal activities of daily living, such as brushing their teeth, eating, showering and dressing." Memory care facilities ensure that these residents get these needs met.

Typically, memory care has a smaller staff-to-patient ratio because a person with dementia has greater care needs. Staff members often have additional training in dementia care as well, though it's important to ask.

Safety is a significant concern for people who may need a memory care facility. In fact, six in 10 people living with dementia will wander at least once in their lives, and many do so repeatedly, according to the Alzheimer's Association[1]. Although common, wandering can be incredibly dangerous, and it's one of the concerns that often weighs most heavily on caregivers and family members.

Memory care facilities have mechanisms in place to prevent wandering, says Pope. "Memory care communities are secured by wander devices [wearable trackers] or locked and alarmed doors," she says. "Most provide outside areas for residents to spend time, but in a safe and secure manner." (Forbes)

SKILLED NURSING HOME CARE-

Skilled care is nursing and therapy care that can only be safely and effectively performed by, or under the supervision of, professionals or technical personnel. Skilled Nursing is health care that is given when you need more involved care to manage, and observe your condition, and evaluate your care. (MEDICARE.GOV)

TRANSITIONAL CARE UNIT (TCU)-

Transitional care: Care involved when a patient/client leaves one care setting (i.e. hospital, nursing home, assisted living facility, SNF, primary care physician, home health, or specialist) and moves to another.

Specifically, they can occur:

1. Within settings; e.g., primary care to specialty care, or intensive care unit (ICU) to ward.
2. Between settings; e.g., hospital to sub-acute care, or ambulatory clinic to senior center.
3. Across health states; e.g., curative care to palliative care or hospice, or personal residence to assisted living.
4. Between providers; e.g., generalist to a specialist practitioner, or acute care provider to a palliative care specialist
5. Transitions of care are a set of actions designed to ensure coordination and continuity. They should be based on a comprehensive care plan and the availability of well-trained practitioners who have current information about the patient's treatment goals, preferences, and health or clinical status. They include logistical arrangements and education of patients and family, as well as coordination among the health professionals involved in the transition.
(www.ntocc.org)
(NACNS.ORG)

Hospice care is a special kind of care that focuses on the quality of life for people who are experiencing an advanced, life-limiting illness and their caregivers. Hospice care provides compassionate care for people in the last phases of incurable disease so that they may live as fully and comfortably as possible.

The hospice philosophy accepts death as the final stage of life: it affirms life, but does not try to hasten or postpone death. Hospice care treats the person and symptoms of the disease, rather than treating the disease itself. A team of professionals work together to manage symptoms so that a person's last days may be spent with dignity and quality, surrounded by their loved ones. Hospice care is also family-centered – it includes the patient and the family in making decisions.

When should hospice care start?

Hospice care is used when a disease, such as advanced cancer, gets to the point when treatment can no longer cure or control it. In general, hospice care should be used when a person is expected to live about 6 months or less if the illness runs its usual course. People with advanced cancer should have a discussion with their family members and doctor to decide together when hospice care should begin.

Studies show hospice care often is not started soon enough. Sometimes the doctor, patient, or family member will resist hospice because they think it means "giving up" or that there's no hope. It's important to know that you can leave hospice and go into active cancer treatment any time you want. But the hope that hospice brings is a quality life, making the best of each day during the last stages of advanced illness.

Some doctors don't bring up hospice, so the patient or family member might decide to start the conversation. If your treatment isn't working anymore and you've run out of treatment options, you might want to ask your doctor or a member of your cancer care team about hospice.

What does hospice care provide?

All hospice providers must offer certain services. But they tend to have different approaches to service, staffing patterns, and types of support services offered. It is important to keep in mind that you can select the Hospice company of your choosing.

Palliative care and symptom control

Palliative care may also be called supportive care, symptom management, or comfort care. It can be given separately from hospice care (for example, while still in active cancer treatment), but It's often a part of hospice care if cancer is no longer being treated because it has worsened. Palliative care does not treat the cancer itself. Instead, it's used to prevent or treat symptoms and side effects as early as possible.

As part of hospice care, palliative care looks at how the cancer experience is affecting the whole person and help to relieve symptoms, pain, and stress. It gives patients options and allows them and their caregivers to take part in planning their care. It's about assuring that all their care needs are addressed. The specialized professionals who are part of the palliative care team can help look for and manage mental, physical, emotional, social, and spiritual issues that may come up.

The main goal of including palliative care into hospice services is to help patients be comfortable while allowing them to enjoy the last stage of life. This means that discomfort, pain, nausea, and other side effects are managed to make sure that you feel as good as possible, yet are alert enough to enjoy the people around you and make important decisions.

Home care and inpatient hospice care

Although most hospice care is centered in the home, there might be times when you need to be in a hospital, extended-care facility, or an inpatient hospice center. Your home hospice team can arrange for inpatient care and will stay involved in your care and with your family. You can go back to in-home care when you and your family are ready. https://www.cancer.org/cancer/end-of-life-care/hospice-care/what-is-hospice-care.html

POLST - POLST is a process and a form

POLST has different names in different states. At the national level, it is simply called **POLST: Portable Medical Orders**, or POLST for short. Portable means that the order is valid outside the clinic or doctor's office, similar to a drug prescription.

POLST is many things, including:

- **A process**. Part of advance care planning, which helps you live the best life possible.
- **A Conversation**. A good talk with your provider about your medical condition, treatment options, and what you want.
- **A medical order form** that travels with you (called a POLST form).

POLST communicates your wishes as medical orders

A POLST form tells **all** health care providers during a medical emergency what you want:

- "Take me to the hospital" or "I want to stay here"
- "Yes, attempt CPR" or "No, don't attempt CPR"
- "These are the medical treatments I want"
- "This is the care plan I want followed"

POLST is for the seriously ill or frail

POLST gives seriously ill or frail people more specific direction over their health care treatments compared to advance directives and more options than Do Not Resuscitate (DNR) orders.

https://polst.org/

Most all states and counties have programs for Seniors to help in guiding them with questions and services that can be utilized, to aid in the coordination of your care, for example in Minnesota, you can contact the Minnesota Department of Health, there are county senior support service telephone lines and there is the Senior Linkage Line, which can help guide the help you need as it pertains to senior care.

Ombudsman- Each State has a Long Term Care Ombudsman office, contact information.

What is an Ombudsman?

The Office of Ombudsman for Long-Term Care (OOLTC) is an independent state agency that serves people needing or receiving long-term care through complaint investigation, advocacy and education.

Resources to Help You

We are committed to providing you with a range of information and resources you can use to advocate for yourself. Our resource page provides various fact sheets, guides, and other resource materials to empower you.

Know Your Rights

OOLTC is dedicated to educating residents and their families on rights, and supporting and empowering residents in exercising their rights. (mn.gov/ooltc)

Contracts and Leases, that are warranted before care or move-in to a Long-Term Care Facility.

Once you have decided on the type of care or which facility is the best fit for your loved one, you will be asked to sign a contract or lease for the apartment. These agreements contain a lot of information that can become confusing and these meetings will seem like you are buying a new home. The complexities within these documents will include things like;

1. POA information
2. Spousal information
3. What are your rights as a resident of a facility, and how do states oversee that you can live in a homelike setting with dignity and purpose?
4. What steps are taken by the facility in the event of a fire, severe weather, an elopement of a resident, and how do they maintain that safety. Drills, fire extinguishers, escape routes and maps.
5. Apartment contents and the responsibility of each party in maintaining the apartment.
6. Who is responsible for what and what are the charges when you move out or pass on? Typically, normal wear and tear is a responsibility of the facility.
7. What types of health services, if any, will be provided such as toileting, bathing or showering, and medication management? What is the cost for that care? Are there any ancillary charges that you will be responsible for, such as nurse visits and support for other conditions that you or your loved one may have, diabetic support, Parkinson's support....
8. Do you need an assistive device for transport, such as a wheelchair, walker? Do you need a 2 person lift to move from bed to chair or chair to bed or toilet? These answers to these questions can be a game changer as to whether the facility can care for you or your loved one.
9. What is the cost for meals and how many meals are included with your care?
10. What type of menus are provided and how does the food taste? It is also advisable to enjoy a meal at the prospective facility, and get an idea of the meal service and palatability of the food. Is it nutritious and tasteful?
11. Is cable TV included or a charge that you will have to pay for?

12. In the event that you go to the hospital, who needs to be contacted by your family so that they are aware of the change in health condition.

13. What types of activities are provided in the community, and have they taken an inventory of the things that you have interest in.

14. What up-front costs and fees are associated with the facility, before moving in?

15. Are there types of health care conditions that facilities will not accept?

16. There may be certain circumstances that you will need to continue your search for other facilities that will accept the care level that is needed.

Does the facility provide on-site health care physicians, nurse practitioners, physician assistants to manage your care, or are you expected to continue using your own physician? This presents an additional problem for some families, because they will be responsible for transportation, unless the facility will provide transportation, which some facilities will do.

Does the facility provide medical emergency pendants so that residents can call for help? What is the cost for that pendant and if lost what is the replacement cost?

Long term care can be quite expensive and before you know it, your life savings can be depleted and if and when that time comes, you need to know what your options are at that time? Who do you talk to and where do you find support for the care that is still needed?

When you notice that funds are getting low, it is important that you discuss with the community administrator about what options are available to you. If the facility has a waiting list for those who need state or government funding, I would advise enrolling in that waiting list as soon as possible, to hopefully continue your care in the same facility that you currently live in. One stressful and avoidable occurrence that can happen, is that your finances are beginning to run low, and you now have to move your loved one to another facility, due to the limited spaces available in the facility for those receiving state or government funded care. Many states but not all states offer assistance when you need it most, so I would advise to contact the state entities in which you live to discover what options available for you or your loved one's care.

These are just a few ideas that you need to think about and not an exhaustive list of everything that needs to be considered. I would advise to really give yourself some time to read, review and ask questions prior to signing the agreement, and ask for a copy so that you can take it home with you, as you want to be as educated as possible.

Questions of concern that you will be asked if your care is required in a Long-Term Care Facility.

How will I afford this type of care if needed- Private pay, or do you need other funding? - Medicaid- Nursing Homes, Elderly Waiver- Assisted living.

Self: _____

Spouse/Significant Other: _____

Notes/Addendums

What does Medicare cover, as it pertains to Home Health, Transitional Care, Assisted Living and Nursing Homes? It is important for you to understand that Medicare only pays for a portion of nursing home costs for a certain period of time, so it is imperative that you educate yourself as to what Medicare actually covers.

Notes/Addendums

133

What does Medicaid cover and what is Medicaid, as it pertains to Home Health, transitional Care, Assisted Living and nursing homes? This step is critical in understanding, what Medicaid covers and how you qualify for financial assistance. I would recommend educating yourself on how to qualify for Medicaid, as this can become very important as your funds are diminishing due to the cost of your care or your loved ones care.

_____

_____

_____

_____

_____

_____

_____

_____

Notes/Addendums

How do I qualify for these services and who do I contact for these services? Most states but not all offer Medicaid or government funding for your care, again you will need to contact your state department of health or local governing agencies to get an understanding of what your current state offers.

Please list those state, local agency numbers below as a reference.

_____

_____

_____

_____

_____

_____

_____

_____

_____

Notes/Addendums

Can I transfer my assets to my beneficiaries and are there consequences for doing this...Look back period- what is the time frame that is allowed by the federal government, currently it is set for a 5 year look back period in almost all states and can vary state by state? If you have transferred assets or gifted money to someone, it may delay your Medicaid eligibility or they may demand that they recover these assets in order for you to qualify for Medicaid Benefits. It is imperative that you speak to a Professional Medicaid Planner or state, local and county case workers.

_____

_____

_____

_____

_____

_____

_____

_____

Notes/Addendums

Religion and Burial Information

What is your religious denomination? Are there any religious/cultural practices limiting health care treatment?

Self: _____

Spouse/Significant Other: _____

Notes/Addendums

What is the name of your church and contact information?

Self: _____

Spouse/Significant Other: _____

Notes/Addendums

What type of burial do you want? Traditional burial (Casket), Cremation?

Self: _____

Spouse/Significant Other: _____

Notes/Addendums

146

Do you have a Burial Insurance Policy? Policy Number, agent, and contact information?

Self: _____

Insurance company:

Address:

Agent Name:

Phone Number:

Policy Number:

Spouse/Significant Other: _____

Insurance company:

Address:

Agent Name:

Phone Number:

Policy Number:

Notes/Addendums

Do you have Pre-paid funeral arrangements, and where is that documentation located?

Self: _____

Spouse/Significant Other: _____

Notes/Addendums

Which funeral home do you prefer, name and contact information?

Self: _____

Funeral Home:

Address:

Phone Number:

Spouse/Significant Other: _____

Funeral Home:

Address:

Phone Number:

Notes/Addendums

Where would you like to be buried if desired- Name of Cemetery and Location? Do you have burial plots that have already been paid for?

Self: _____

Cemetery Name:

Location, City, State:

Contact Phone Number:

Plots Paid for:

Spouse/Significant Other: _____

Cemetery Name:

Location, City, State:

Contact Phone Number:

Plots Paid for:

Notes/Addendums

154

Burial Funeral Wishes

Do you have an outfit that you have picked out for your funeral? Do you have particular songs or a musician that you would like to perform at your funeral, that your family or loved one's should know about? Do you have favorite flowers that you would like to have at the place of your burial ceremony?

Notes/Addendums

157

Conclusion

We would like to begin with thanking you for purchasing this interactive workbook. The information that you have provided will help you and your loved ones in the event that this information is needed. We recommend updating this book as mentioned, to keep it current with any changes in your information. It is also to be understood that if you have any questions regarding a particular subject in this book, that there are state agencies that you can refer to or an attorney who can assist you in gathering the answers to some of your questions. We have tried to simplify this book in order to assist you in answering the needed questions in the event of a change in health. You have helped paint a clear picture of your wishes, for you and your loved one's.

Thank you again,
Michael White LNHA,LALD and Lisa White RN

Made in the USA
Monee, IL
27 October 2024